SMALL GROUP STUDY

LAUGH YOUR WAY to a BETTER MARRIAGE® SMALL GROUP STUDY
Published by Laugh Your Way America! LLC

©2008, 2010, 2011 by Laugh Your Way America! LLC
International Standard Book Number: 978-1-935519-21-8
Mark Gungor, author

ALL RIGHTS RESERVED
No part of this publication may be reproduced, stored in a retrieval system,
or transmitted, in any form or by any means-electronic, mechanical, photocopying,
recording, or otherwise-without prior written permission.

ACKNOWLEDGEMENTS

To Diane Brierley, for her work in writing this study guide.

To Phil Gungor for his editing and production of the accompanying DVD.

TABLE OF CONTENTS	PAGE
HOW TO USE THIS STUDY GUIDE	6
INTRODUCTION	7
SESSION 1: WHAT'S NORMAL?	
Clip 1 - Trouble (4:40)	8
Clip 2 - Stereotypes (2:11)	10
Clip 3 - Cultural Perceptions of Marriage (2:28)	12
Clip 4 - Relational Physics (1:35)	14
SESSION 2: MEN'S BRAINS…WOMEN'S BRAINS	
Clip 5 - Boxes vs. Wires (7:51)	16
Clip 6 - Handling Stress (5:18)	18
Clip 7 - RAM and Details (3:06)	20
SESSION 3: FEW VS. MANY	
Clip 8 - Words (5:51)	22
Clip 9 - Single Tasking vs. Multi-Tasking (16:48)	24
SESSION 4: FORMULA FOR SUCCESS	
Clip 10 - Smiley Face (12:48)	26
SESSION 5: TEACH AN OLD DOG…	
Clip 11 - Give and Take (5:05)	29
Clip 12 - Ask More Than Once (8:55)	31
Clip 13 - Ask the Right Way (1:10)	32
SESSION 6: NEW TRICKS	
Clip 14 - Train Him (5:31)	34
Clip 15 - Barter (5:32)	36
Clip 16 - Conditional Relationships (7:29)	37
SESSION 7: THE PRINCESS AND THE WARRIOR	
Clip 17 - Self-Esteem (10:01)	40
Clip 18 - Go Back for the Girl (10:59)	42
SESSION 8: SEX: THE MIND GAME	
Clip 19 - Variables (12:14)	45
Clip 20 - Focus on the Girl (1:06)	47
Clip 21 - Romance (7:13)	48
SESSION 9: SEX: WHAT MATTERS	
Clip 22 - Foreplay (4:39)	50
Clip 23 - Time (6:45)	52
Clip 24 - Privacy (6:36)	54
SESSION 10: THE #1 KEY TO INCREDIBLE SEX	
Clip 25 - Exclusivity and Lust (17:23)	56
Clip 26 - Scientific Formula for the Best Possible Sex (17:37)	58
SESSION 11: SCORE!	
Clip 27 - Men Scoring Points (11:19)	61
Clip 28 - Women Scoring Points (4:29)	63
SESSION 12: STARTING OVER…AGAIN	
Clip 29 - The Reset Button (8:36)	65
Clip 30 - Forgiveness (2:45)	66
Clip 31 - The Story of Bathsheba (3:34)	68
Clip 32 - Pushing the Reset Button (2:47)	72

www.laughyourway.com

HOW TO USE THIS STUDY GUIDE

This study guide contains a series of questions for discussion that follow video clips taken from Mark Gungor's weekend seminar, Laugh Your Way to a Better Marriage®. It can be used by individual couples or as a small group study to strengthen, improve and enrich marriages. It's also a perfect follow-up study to a Laugh Your Way to a Better Marriage® event.

The 32 video clips, varying in length, are divided into twelve sessions. Scripture references and discussion questions are listed for all clips. Each session includes a prayer that couples or leaders can use in closing.

Session lengths will vary depending on the size of your group and the amount of discussion generated. Allow between 60-90 minutes per meeting. You may find that your group has extended discussions and that it will take longer to complete the entire study. Adjust the sessions according to the needs of your group.

This study is designed so that group leaders use the study guide and DVDs to conduct the group. Each person or couple has their own study guide to take notes and write in answers. This workbook is copyrighted and may not be reproduced.

IMPORTANT NOTE IN REGARD TO SESSIONS 4 AND 8-10

A portion of the Laugh Your Way to a Better Marriage® small group study is devoted to the sexual relationship side of marriage. We recommend that group leaders preview this section of the study to see if it is a good fit for your group. Some groups may decide to skip this section. Others may want to watch the clips together but save the discussion questions for couples to go through together at home in a more private setting. There may be some groups that feel they can proceed through these sections as written. Feel free to handle this portion as you deem appropriate.

ATTENTION SMALL GROUP LEADERS!

Please take a few minutes to register your small group with us. We will have record of all of the small groups using this study and will be able to notify you of updates or other small group materials as they become available.

Please go to www.laughyourway.com and under the "Resources" menu,
click on "Small Groups" to register.

PLEASE NOTE THAT
LAUGH YOUR WAY TO A BETTER MARRIAGE®: SMALL GROUP STUDY GUIDE
IS COPYRIGHTED AND MAY NOT BE REPRODUCED.

www.laughyourway.com

INTRODUCTION

It takes wisdom to have a good family, and it takes understanding to make it strong. It takes knowledge to fill a home with rare and beautiful treasures. Wise people have great power, and those with knowledge have great strength. Proverbs 24:3-5 (NCV)

Marriage is wonderful, complicated, fulfilling, stressful, exhilarating and a hundred other things…sometimes all at the same time! There are times of intense joy and times of great frustration. Husbands and wives experience many ups/downs and highs/lows during the process of growing together in their marriage. Often times, the difficulties and struggles that arise seem daunting and couples feel as if they are the only ones this happens to. The challenges can seem overwhelming.

In his Laugh Your Way to a Better Marriage® seminar, Mark Gungor tackles some of the most common challenges that married couples face. He uses humor to unravel the complexities of marriage and reveals biblical truths to help husbands and wives gain the knowledge and understanding needed to build a healthier, stronger and more fulfilling marriage. They discover that they are not the only ones who have issues and that they are not alone!

SESSION 1 - What's Normal?

CLIP 1: TROUBLE (4:40)

The Bible is clear that problems are a part of marriage. Why then, do couples get upset when they experience trouble?

What are some of the unrealistic expectations husbands and wives can have of their marriage and each other?

How do you and your spouse handle the "positive" and the "pooh" in your marriage? What do you think your "positive to pooh" ratio is?

SCRIPTURE REFERENCES:

Proverbs 14:4
Where there are no oxen, the manger is empty, but from the strength of an ox comes abundant harvest. (NIV)

Ecclesiastes 4:9-12
Two people can accomplish more than twice as much as one; they get a better return for their labor. [10]If one person falls, the other can reach out and help. But people who are alone when they fall are in real trouble. [11]And on a cold night, two under the same blanket can gain warmth from each other. But how can one be warm alone? [12]A person standing alone can be attacked and defeated, but two can stand back-to-back and conquer. Three are even better, for a triple-braided cord is not easily broken. (NLT)

1 Corinthians 7:1
Now for the matters you wrote about: It is good for a man not to marry. (NIV)

www.laughyourway.com

1 Corinthians 7:28
But those who marry will face many troubles in this life, and I want to spare you this. (NIV)

NOTES:

Two people can accomplish more than twice as much as one; they get a better return for their labor.

Ecclesiastes 4:9

CLIP 2: STEREOTYPES (2:11)

What are some of the stereotypes about men and women that are common in our culture today?

In what ways do you and your spouse fit the standard male/female stereotypes?

In what ways are you different from those stereotypes?

What are some problems that you have experienced in your marriage in regard to stereotypes?

SCRIPTURE REFERENCES:

Proverbs 3:13-18
[13]Happy is the person who finds wisdom and gains understanding.[14]For the profit of wisdom is better than silver, and her wages are better than gold. [15]Wisdom is more precious than rubies; nothing you desire can compare with her. [16]She offers you life in her right hand, and riches and honor in her left. [17]She will guide you down delightful paths; all her ways are satisfying. [18]Wisdom is a tree of life to those who embrace her; happy are those who hold her tightly. (NLT)

Philippians 1:9
I pray that your love for each other will overflow more and more, and that you will keep on growing in your knowledge and understanding. (NLT)

NOTES:

I pray that your love for each other will overflow more and more, and that you will keep on growing in your knowledge and understanding.

Philippians 1:9

CLIP 3: CULTURAL PERCEPTIONS (2:28)

In general, our culture's perception of marriage is that it's a "life-sucking" institution. How is this reflected in the world around us?

In what ways is marriage portrayed as "life-giving"?

Statistics show that married people live longer, are healthier, wealthier, happier, and have better sex. Why do you think this is true?

How does the media feed the myth that single people are the ones who "have it made" and that married people are often miserable?

SCRIPTURE REFERENCES:

Genesis 2:18-24
[18] The LORD God said, "It is not good for the man to be alone. I will make a helper suitable for him." [19] Now the LORD God had formed out of the ground all the beasts of the field and all the birds of the air. He brought them to the man to see what he would name them; and whatever the man called each living creature, that was its name. [20] So the man gave names to all the livestock, the birds of the air and all the beasts of the field. But for Adam no suitable helper was found. [21] So the LORD God

caused the man to fall into a deep sleep; and while he was sleeping, he took one of the man's ribs and closed up the place with flesh. ²² Then the LORD God made a woman from the rib he had taken out of the man, and he brought her to the man. ²³ The man said, "This is now bone of my bones and flesh of my flesh; she shall be called 'woman,' for she was taken out of man." ²⁴ For this reason a man will leave his father and mother and be united to his wife, and they will become one flesh. (NIV)

Proverbs 18:22
He who finds a wife finds a good thing, and gets favor from the Lord. (NLT)

Proverbs 19:14
Parents can provide their sons with an inheritance of houses and wealth, but only the LORD can give an understanding wife. (NLT)

Proverbs 27:17
As iron sharpens iron, so people can improve each other. (NCV)

Proverbs 31:11-12
¹¹ Her husband can trust her, and she will greatly enrich his life. ¹² She will not hinder him but help him all her life. (NLT)

NOTES:

He who finds a wife finds a good thing, and gets favor from the Lord.

Proverbs 18:22

www.laughyourway.com

CLIP 4: RELATIONAL PHYSICS (1:35)

In what areas of marriage are couples in our culture "clueless" about today? Why do you think this is so?

Why do you think Christians can have miserable marriages, while non-Christians can have great marriages?

What rules of "relational physics" do you think couples break in their marriages? What is the result of breaking the rules?

SCRIPTURE REFERENCES:

Proverbs 3:13
Blessed is the man who finds wisdom, the man who gains understanding. (NIV)

Proverbs 4:5-7
[5] Sell everything and buy wisdom! Forage for understanding! Don't forget one word! Don't deviate an inch! [6] Never walk away from wisdom—she guards your life; love her - she keeps her eye on you. [7] Above all and before all, do this: Get wisdom! Write this at the top of your list: Get understanding! (MSG)

www.laughyourway.com

NOTES:

END OF SESSION PRAYER

GROUP PRAYER:

Father,
Help us to grow in understanding of each other. Help us to learn your design for marriage. Give us a spirit of oneness and unity and help us to complete one another as Your word says we were created to do. Keep us ever mindful of the ways we think about and perceive our marriage and each other. Help us to be real with our spouses and think realistically in what our relationship should be about. Surround us with friends and family who will support and uphold our marriage and all marriages as the wonderful, life-giving union you intended it to be. Amen.

COUPLES PRAYER:

Father,
Help us to grow in understanding of each other. Help us to learn Your design for marriage. Give us a spirit of oneness and unity and help us to complete one another as your word says we were created to do. Keep us ever mindful of the ways we think about and perceive our marriage and each other. Help us to be real with each other and think realistically in what our relationship should be about. Surround us with friends and family who will support and uphold our marriage as the wonderful, life-giving union you intend it to be. Amen.

Blessed is the man who finds wisdom, the man who gains understanding.

Proverbs 3:13

SESSION 2 - Men's Brains...Women's Brains

CLIP 5: BOXES VS. WIRES (7:51)

How are men's and women's brains different from each other?

Give examples from your own marriage that demonstrate these differences.

What situations in your marriage does the concept of "The Nothing Box" help to explain?

SCRIPTURE REFERENCES:

Proverbs 1:5
The wise also will hear and increase in learning, and the person of understanding will acquire skill and attain to sound counsel so that he may be able to steer his course rightly. (AMP)

Proverbs 20:5
Someone's thoughts may be as deep as the ocean, but if you are smart, you will discover them. (CEV)

www.laughyourway.com

NOTES:

> *Someone's thoughts may be as deep as the ocean, but if you are smart, you will discover them.*
>
> *Proverbs 20:5*

CLIP 6: HANDLING STRESS (5:18)

How do men and women handle stress differently?

In what ways is this true of you and your spouse?

Knowing these differences, how can you and your spouse best support each other during times of stress and conflict?

SCRIPTURE REFERENCES:

Psalm 49:3
My mouth will speak words of wisdom; the utterance from my heart will give understanding. (NIV)

Proverbs 2:2
Tune your ears to wisdom, and concentrate on understanding. (NIV)

NOTES:

My mouth will speak words of wisdom; the utterance from my heart will give understanding.

Psalm 49:3

CLIP 7: RAM/DETAILS (3:06)

Do you and your spouse fit this classic stereotype of remembering details?

What problems has this caused in your relationship?

What steps can you take to accommodate this difference?

SCRIPTURE REFERENCES:

Proverbs 9:6
Forsake all thoughtlessness and live; walk in the way of understanding.

Proverbs 18:15
The mind of a person with understanding gets knowledge; the wise person listens to learn more. (NCV)
Wise men and women are always learning, always listening for fresh insights. (MSG)

www.laughyourway.com

NOTES:

END OF SESSION PRAYER

GROUP PRAYER AND COUPLES PRAYER:

Father,
Bless each marriage and family represented here. Give us open hearts and minds to hear what You want us to hear. Guide us in gaining wisdom and understanding of the differences between each other. Help us learn to appreciate and respect those differences in order to build a deep and rich marriage relationship. Make us forever grateful for the person You have blessed each of us with as a mate. Amen.

Forsake all thoughtlessness, and live; and walk in the way of understanding.

Proverbs 9:6

SESSION 3 - Few vs. Many

CLIP 8: WORDS (5:51)

What differences are there between men and women in the way they use words?

In your marriage, is there one person who requires more words?

What problems can this difference between men and women cause in a marriage?

Can you list any words or actions that you and your spouse have different meanings for?

What can happen as a result of having different meanings?

What steps can you take to deal with the frustration that may be caused by the different meanings of your words?

SCRIPTURE REFERENCES:

Psalm 49:3
My mouth will speak words of wisdom; the utterance from my heart will give understanding. (NIV)

Proverbs 2:2
Tune your ears to wisdom and concentrate on understanding. (NIV)

Proverbs 18:4
The words of a man's mouth are deep waters; the fountain of wisdom is a gushing stream. (RSV)

Proverbs 17:27
He who restrains his words has knowledge, and he who has a cool spirit is a man of understanding. (NASB)

NOTES:

My mouth will speak words of wisdom; the utterance from my heart will give understanding.

Psalm 49:3

CLIP 9: SINGLE TASKING VS. MULTI-TASKING (16:48)

Explain how you and your spouse fit the single and multi-tasking roles.

Taking into account the differences in how men and women listen, name some instances when these differences may have interfered with communication in your marriage.

What things could each of you do to improve the way you communicate?

SCRIPTURE REFERENCES:

Proverbs 19:20
Listen to counsel and receive instruction that you may eventually become wise. (NAB)

Philippians 2:2
Then make me truly happy by agreeing wholeheartedly with each other, loving one another, and working together with one heart and purpose. (NLT)

NOTES:

www.laughyourway.com

END OF SESSION PRAYER

GROUP PRAYER:

Father,
Thank you for the growing understanding we have of our mates. Help us to be wise and to truly listen and hear what our husbands and our wives are saying to us. Guide our hearts and help us to speak wisely in our families. Give us a single spirit of unity to work together to create a peaceful and loving home. Help us also be the kind of husbands and wives that will model and reflect Your love and Your light to the world around us. Amen.

COUPLES PRAYER:

Father,
Thank you for the growing understanding we have of each other. Help us to be wise and to truly listen and hear what we say to each other. Guide our hearts and help us to speak wisely in our family. Give us a single spirit of unity to work together to create a peaceful and loving home. Help us to also be the kind of husband and wife that will model and reflect Your love and Your light to the world around us. Amen.

Listen to counsel and receive instruction, that you may eventually become wise.

Proverbs 19:20

www.laughyourway.com

SESSION 4 - Formula for Success

CLIP 10: SMILEY FACE (12:48)

Testosterone is largely responsible for the male sex drive. How does this help you to understand the different ways men and women think about sex?

Wives, what things can your husband do to "touch your heart"?

Husbands, is physical intimacy the key to emotional intimacy for you?

How does not having regular sex or cutting off sex from your husband work against your relationship?

www.laughyourway.com

How does the "smiley face/heart" system Mark demonstrated explain God's design for a marriage relationship? How has this system been misunderstood by both husbands and wives?

How does giving your spouse what he/she wants help you to get what you want?

SCRIPTURE REFERENCES:

Proverbs 27:19
As one face differs from another, so does one human heart from another. (NAB)

1 Corinthians 7:3
The marriage bed must be a place of mutuality - the husband seeking to satisfy his wife, the wife seeking to satisfy her husband. (MSG)

NOTES:

The marriage bed must be a place of mutuality - the husband seeking to satisfy his wife, the wife seeking to satisfy her husband.

1 Corinthians 7:3

END OF SESSION PRAYER

GROUP PRAYER:

Father,
We ask for Your guidance and wisdom in understanding the physical part of our relationship. Help us to learn and follow the plan You created for us. Open our hearts to the keys we need to unlock this most intimate part of our marriage. Create a spirit in each of us so we can give to and fulfill the desires of our husbands and wives hearts. Strengthen us as husbands, wives and lovers. Amen.

COUPLES PRAYER:

Father,
We ask for Your guidance and wisdom in understanding the physical part of our relationship. Help us to learn and follow the plan You created for us. Open our hearts to the keys we need to unlock this most intimate part of our marriage. Create a spirit in each of us so we can give to and fulfill the desires of each other's heart. Strengthen us as a husband and wife and as lovers. Amen

SESSION 5 - Teach an Old Dog...

CLIP 11: GIVE AND TAKE (5:05)

In what ways are you and your spouse like the typical "givers and takers"?

What problems have you experienced related to giving and taking in your marriage?

What makes women uncomfortable with taking? How can they learn to take or extract things from their husbands?

What can you do to create a relationship in which the give and take between you is more balanced?

Are there any "false romantic fantasies" that you have about your relationship?

www.laughyourway.com

SCRIPTURE REFERENCES:

Proverbs 11:17
A kind man benefits himself, but a cruel man brings trouble on himself. (NIV)

Proverbs 11:24
One person gives freely, yet gains more; another withholds what is right, only to become poor. (CSB)

Proverbs 11:25
The man who gives much will have much, and he who helps others will be helped himself. (NLV)

Ecclesiastes 11:1
Give generously, for your gifts will return to you later. (NLT)

NOTES:

CLIP 12: ASK MORE THAN ONCE (8:55)

Can you think of situations in your marriage when having to ask more than once caused a problem?

Women, how does it make you feel to have to ask more than once?

Men, do you need to be asked more than once?

What problems are caused by "judging the motivations" of why men do things?

How do husbands and wives set themselves up in this area? What steps can you take to end the frustration?

SCRIPTURE REFERENCES:

Proverbs 15:1
A gentle response defuses anger, but a sharp tongue kindles a temper-fire. (MSG)

Proverbs 25:15
Patient persistence pierces through indifference; gentle speech breaks down rigid defenses. (MSG)

One person gives freely, yet gains more; another withholds what is right, only to become poor.

Proverbs 11:24

www.laughyourway.com

NOTES:

CLIP 13: ASK THE RIGHT WAY (1:10)

What is the right way to ask? What is the wrong way to ask?

How do men and women respond differently to insult?

Husbands, what way of asking is most motivating to you?

SCRIPTURE REFERENCES:

Proverbs 12:18
Rash language cuts and maims, but there is healing in the words of the wise. (MSG)

Proverbs 16:24
Pleasant words are like a honeycomb, making people happy and healthy. (NCV)

Proverbs 18:21
Words kill, words give life; they're either poison or fruit - you choose. (MSG)

NOTES:

END OF SESSION PRAYER

GROUP PRAYER:

*Father,
Give us patient and persistent hearts as we continue to grow and learn about our differences. Help us to treat our husbands and wives according to what they need and what is best for them. As Your word says, teach us how to set ourselves aside, to die to ourselves and to put our spouses first. Amen.*

COUPLES PRAYER:

*Father,
Give us patient and persistent hearts as we continue to grow and learn about our differences. Help us to treat one another according to what the other needs and what is best for them. As Your word says, teach us how to set ourselves aside, to die to ourselves and to put our spouse first. Amen.*

Patient persistence pierces through indifference; gentle speech breaks down rigid defenses.

Proverbs 25:15

www.laughyourway.com

SESSION 6 - New Tricks

CLIP 14: TRAIN HIM (5:31)

Wives, in what ways have you seen positive reinforcement work with your husband?

Husbands, how does appreciation and positive reinforcement feel to you?

What are some behaviors that wives view as "expected" from their husbands?

What are some acts of "unexpected kindness" that women appreciate?

SCRIPTURE REFERENCES:

Proverbs 9:9
Give teaching to a wise man and he will be even wiser. Teach a man who is right and good, and he will grow in learning. (NLV)

Proverbs 15:23
Joy comes to a man with the reply of his mouth. How good is a word at the right time! (WEB)

Proverbs 16:23
Wise people's minds tell them what to say, and that helps them be better teachers. (NCV)

NOTES:

CLIP 15: BARTER (5:32)

How do you feel about bartering for things in your relationship?

What are some things that you could barter for with each other?

Do you think that using sex as a bartering tool is ok? Why or why not?

SCRIPTURE REFERENCES:

Proverbs 12:14
People can get many good things by the words they say; the work of their hands also gives them many benefits. (NLT)

Proverbs 16:23
You can persuade others if you are wise and speak sensibly. (CEV)

NOTES:

Give teaching to a wise man and he will be even wiser. Teach a man who is right and good, and he will grow in learning.

Proverbs 9:9

CLIP 16: CONDITIONAL RELATIONSHIPS (7:29)

What kind of "faulty" information has been given to women in the area of conditional relationships?

Why does a healthy relationship demand conditions? What happens if there are NO conditions?

What examples from the Bible can you think of that show God has conditions?

Why must you be careful with how you handle the conditions in your relationships?

SCRIPTURE REFERENCES:

Matthew 6:15
But if you do not forgive men their sins, your Father will not forgive your sins. (NIV)

John 3:16
For God so loved the world that He gave His one and only Son, that whoever believes in Him shall not perish but have eternal life. (NIV)

James 4:8a
Come near to God and He will come near to you. (NIV)

www.laughyourway.com

NOTES:

END OF SESSION PRAYER

GROUP PRAYER:

Father,
Thank you for the blessing You have given us in our husbands and wives. May we always have a deep sense of appreciation for who You created that person to be. Help us to show one another that appreciation as well as unexpected kindness and love. Give us the perseverance to keep on and the patience to view our marriages in the long-term. Show us how to bring joy to our spouse and find the joy in our lives together in some small way each and every day. Amen.

COUPLES PRAYER:

Father,
Thank you for the blessing You have given us in each other as husband and wife. May we always have a deep sense of appreciation for who You created this person to be. Help us to show one another that appreciation as well as unexpected kindness and love. Give us the perseverance to keep on and the patience to view our marriage in the long-term. Show us how to bring joy to one another and to find the joy in our lives together in some small way each and every day. Amen.

www.laughyourway.com

Pride only breeds quarrels, but wisdom is found in those who take advice.

Proverbs 13:10

SESSION 7 - The Princess and the Warrior

CLIP 17: SELF-ESTEEM (10:01)

In what ways do each of you fit the generalizations about male and female self-esteem?

Husbands, what qualities do you find most attractive about your wife?

How does the media and our culture impact our perception of beauty?

Wives, what things can you do to improve your self-image and self-esteem?

www.laughyourway.com

Husbands, how can you support your wife and help her with this?

Why is confidence so important?

SCRIPTURE REFERENCES:

Proverbs 15:13
A joyful heart makes a cheerful face, but when the heart is sad, the spirit is broken. (NASB)

Song of Solomon 7:1-6
[1] How beautiful your sandaled feet, O prince's daughter! Your graceful legs are like jewels, the work of a craftsman's hands. [2] Your navel is a rounded goblet that never lacks blended wine. Your waist is a mound of wheat encircled by lilies. [3] Your breasts are like two fawns, twins of a gazelle. [4] Your neck is like an ivory tower. Your eyes are the pools of Heshbon by the gate of Bath Rabbim. Your nose is like the tower of Lebanon looking toward Damascus. [5] Your head crowns you like Mount Carmel. Your hair is like royal tapestry; the king is held captive by its tresses. [6] How beautiful you are and how pleasing, O love, with your delights! (NIV)

NOTES:

CLIP 18: GO BACK FOR THE GIRL (10:59)

What is in the heart of every man? Husbands, do you agree? Wives, do you see this in your husband?

What is in the heart of every woman? Wives, do you agree? Husbands do you see this in your wife?

In your marriage, is your wife the handbook on relationships? How can you take advantage of the benefits of this is in your relationship?

Why is it so important that a husband "goes back for the girl"?

Wives, what does this mean to you? What does your husband need to do in order to show he is "rescuing you"?

What keeps husbands from "going back for the girl"?

What constitutes a "real" man?

SCRIPTURE REFERENCES:

Proverbs 13:10
Pride only breeds quarrels, but wisdom is found in those who take advice. (NIV)

Proverbs 13:12
Not getting what you want can make you feel sick, but a wish that comes true is a life-giving tree. (CEV)

Proverbs 13:16
Wise people think before they act. (NLT)

Proverbs 19:22
What is desired in a man is his kindness… (NLV)

NOTES:

A joyful heart makes a cheerful face, but when the heart is sad, the spirit is broken.

Proverbs 15:13

END OF SESSION PRAYER

GROUP PRAYER:

Father,
We know that Your word says we are created in Your image. Help us to have eyes to see the true beauty and wonder You created in each of us. Let us always look at ourselves and our mates through Your eyes, rather than the eyes of the world around us. Give us self-confidence to know that we are indeed fearfully and wonderfully made. May we always love and esteem one another in word and action. Help us to truly discover what is hidden in one another's hearts. Give us patience and wisdom to seek out and meet the needs of our husbands and wives. Give men strength and courage to fight their battles and the heart to rescue their beauty and go back for their girl. Amen.

COUPLES PRAYER:

Father,
We know that Your word says we are created in Your image. Help us to have eyes to see the true beauty and wonder You created in both of us. Let us always look at ourselves and each other through Your eyes, rather than the eyes of the world around us. Give us self-confidence to know that we are indeed fearfully and wonderfully made. May we always love and esteem one another in word and action. Amen.

COUPLES PRAYER: (WIFE TO PRAY)

Father,
Help us to truly discover what is hidden in one another's hearts. Give us patience and wisdom to seek out and meet the needs of each other. Give my husband strength and courage to fight his battles and give him the heart to rescue me, his beauty, and always go back for his girl. Amen.

www.laughyourway.com

SESSION 8 - Sex: The Mind Game

CLIP 19: VARIABLES (12:14)

What are some variables that can have an influence on the sexual relationship in a marriage?

What are the consequences of "lust-filled" imprinting, especially on men?

Why is it so important that our first sexual experiences cause us to imprint on the girl?

Why do you think that people who wait until they are married to have sex have a fraction of the divorce rate of those who don't?

> *Husbands, go all out in your love for your wives, exactly as Christ did for the church - a love marked by giving, not getting.*
>
> *Ephesians 5:25*

What are the consequences of pre-marital sex on the woman's imprinting process?

How can this be problematic in a marriage? How do you best deal with these variables in a marriage?

Why is it so vitally important that our children get the correct information about sex, rather than the lies that our culture feeds them?

SCRIPTURE REFERENCES:

1 Corinthians 7:3-5
³The marriage bed must be a place of mutuality - the husband seeking to satisfy his wife, the wife seeking to satisfy her husband. ⁴ Marriage is not a place to "stand up for your rights." Marriage is a decision to serve the other, whether in bed or out. ⁵ Abstaining from sex is permissible for a period of time if you both agree to, and if it is for the purposes of prayer and fasting - but only for such times. Then come back together again. Satan has an ingenious way of tempting us when we least expect it. (MSG)

Hebrews 13:4
Marriage should be honored by all and the marriage bed kept pure; for God will judge the adulterer and all the sexually immoral. (NIV)

NOTES:

CLIP 20: FOCUS ON THE GIRL (1:06)

Why is it so important to focus on the woman in the physical relationship?

Is communicating about the sexual aspect of marriage more difficult and uncomfortable than other areas? Why is that so?

SCRIPTURE REFERENCES:

Proverbs 5:18-19
[18] May your fountain be blessed, and may you rejoice in the wife of your youth. [19] A loving doe, a graceful deer - may her breasts satisfy you always, may you ever be captivated by her love. (NIV)

Song of Solomon 7:10-13
[10] I belong to my lover, and his desire is for me. [11] Come, my lover, let us go to the countryside, let us spend the night in the villages. [12] Let us go early to the vineyards to see if the vines have budded, if their blossoms have opened, and if the pomegranates are in bloom- there I will give you my love. [13] The mandrakes send out their fragrance, and at our door is every delicacy, both new and old, that I have stored up for you, my lover. (NIV)

NOTES:

How beautiful you are and how pleasing, O love, with your delights!

Song of Solomon 7:6

---

www.laughyourway.com

CLIP 21: ROMANCE (7:13)

How has pornography changed how people (especially men) view the role of romance in the sexual relationship?

How does the "desire required up front" model cause problems in marriages?

Why is "who initiates sex" a big issue in so many marriages?

SCRIPTURE REFERENCES:

Song of Solomon 4:10
How delightful is your love, my sister, my bride! How much more pleasing is your love than wine, and the fragrance of your perfume than any spice! (NIV)

Ephesians 5:25-28
[25] Husbands, go all out in your love for your wives, exactly as Christ did for the church - a love marked by giving, not getting. [26] Christ's love makes the church whole. His words evoke her beauty. Everything He does and says is designed to bring the best out of her, [27] dressing her in dazzling white silk, radiant with holiness. [28] And that is how husbands ought to love their wives. They're really doing themselves a favor - since they're already "one" in marriage. (MSG)

www.laughyourway.com

NOTES:

END OF SESSION PRAYER

GROUP PRAYER:

Father,
We ask that You give us guidance and wisdom regarding the sexual part of our marriages. We know that You have created the perfect plan for intimacy in marriage. Help us to discover and follow that plan to enrich our relationships. God, we ask for healing among those of us who need it in the areas where we may have done things wrong to begin with. You are the Great Healer and Restorer. Forgive us, Father, for those things which were done in the past that may be affecting our lives and our marriages today. Bring understanding and restoration to the deepest parts of our lives and marriages. Give us the patience and courage to make the adjustments necessary to have fulfilling, intimate marriages. Amen.

COUPLES PRAYER:

Father,
We ask that You give us guidance and wisdom regarding the sexual part of our marriage. We know that You have created the perfect plan for intimacy in marriage. Help us to discover and follow that plan to enrich our relationship. God, we ask for healing for the areas where we have done things wrong to begin with. You are the Great Healer and Restorer. Forgive us, Father, for those things which were done in the past that may be affecting our lives and our marriage today. Bring understanding and restoration to the deepest parts of our lives and marriage. Give us the patience and courage to make the adjustments necessary to have a fulfilling, intimate marriage. Amen.

www.laughyourway.com

How beautiful you are, my darling; there is no flaw in you.

Song of Solomon 4:7

SESSION 9 - Sex: What Matters

CLIP 22: FOREPLAY (4:39)

According to Mark's advice, what things can husbands do that wives would consider "foreplay"?

How do men's and women's ideas of "foreplay" differ?

Why is it so important to wives that their husbands take the time to "climb the palm tree"?

What things can husbands do to keep their sexual relationship from becoming predictable and formulaic?

SCRIPTURE REFERENCES:

Song of Solomon 4:15-16
[15] You are a garden fountain, a well of flowing water streaming down from Lebanon. [16] Awake, north wind, and come, south wind! Blow on my garden, that its fragrance may spread abroad. Let my lover come into his garden and taste its choice fruits. (NIV)

Song of Solomon 7:6-9
[6] How beautiful you are and how pleasing, O love, with your delights! [7] Your stature is like that of the palm, and your breasts like clusters of fruit. [8] I said, "I will climb the palm tree; I will take hold of its fruit." May your breasts be like the clusters of the vine, the fragrance of your breath like apples, [9] and your mouth like the best wine. (NIV)

NOTES:

Above all else, guard your heart, for it is the wellspring of life.

Proverbs 4:23

www.laughyourway.com

CLIP 23: TIME (6:45)

Why is time such an important factor in creating a satisfying sexual relationship?

What are the effects when husbands take shortcuts in this area?

What is the definition of a lover? How do husbands benefit when they really take on this role?

What can wives do to help their husbands become more skilled in the "time" area of sex?

SCRIPTURE REFERENCES:

Song of Solomon 2:16-17
[16] My lover is mine, and I am his. Nightly he strolls in our garden, delighting in the flowers [17] until dawn breathes its light and night slips away. Turn to me, dear lover. Come like a gazelle. Leap like a wild stag on delectable mountains! (MSG)

Song of Solomon 4:1-7
[1] How beautiful you are, my darling! Oh, how beautiful! Your eyes behind your veil are doves. Your hair is like a flock of goats descending from Mount Gilead. [2] Your teeth are like a flock of sheep just shorn, coming up from the washing. Each has its twin; not one of them is alone. [3] Your lips are like a scarlet ribbon; your mouth is lovely. Your temples behind your veil are like the halves of a pomegranate. [4] Your neck is like the tower of David, built with elegance; on it hang a thousand shields, all of them shields of warriors. [5] Your two breasts are like two fawns, like twin fawns of a gazelle that browse among the lilies. [6] Until the day breaks and the shadows flee, I will go to the mountain of myrrh and to the hill of incense. [7] How beautiful you are, my darling; there is no flaw in you. (NIV)

NOTES:

I belong to my lover, and his desire is for me.

Song of Solomon 7:10

www.laughyourway.com

CLIP 24: PRIVACY (6:36)

Why is privacy so important – especially for women – when it comes to sex?

How do women change when they become mothers? How do these changes impact their marriage relationship?

Why is using motherhood as an excuse to put marriage on hold so dangerous to the relationship?

What kind of plans can couples make to arrange private time away from their children in order to maintain their marriage? Why is this so important?

Why is the rejection factor such a huge deal to men?

SCRIPTURE REFERENCES:

Song of Solomon 7:11-12

[11] Come, my lover, let us go to the countryside, let us spend the night in the villages. [12] Let us go early to the vineyards to see if the vines have budded, if their blossoms have opened, and if the pomegranates are in bloom. There I will give you my love. (NIV)

NOTES:

END OF SESSION PRAYER

GROUP PRAYER:

Father,
Help us to learn what it takes to have a closer and more intimate marriage, the way You designed it to be. Give us patience and wisdom as we grow and discover what it takes to romance our husbands and wives. Bless our marriages and the time we spend together. Help us to become more and more aware of what our spouses need from us and give us hearts that desire to unselfishly fulfill those needs for them. Show us how to love each other completely and unconditionally as You love us. Amen.

COUPLES PRAYER:

Father,
Help us to learn what it takes to have a closer and more intimate marriage, the way You designed it to be. Give us patience and wisdom as we grow and discover what it takes to romance one another. Bless our marriage and the time we spend together. Help us to become more and more aware of each other's needs and give us hearts that desire to unselfishly fulfill those desires. Show us how to love each other completely and unconditionally as You love us. Amen.

www.laughyourway.com

How delightful is your love, my sister, my bride! How much more pleasing is your love than wine, and the fragrance of your perfume than any spice!

Song of Solomon 4:10

SESSION 10 - The #1 Key to Incredible Sex

CLIP 25: EXCLUSIVITY AND LUST (17:23)

What is it about exclusivity that makes it the "# 1 Key to Incredible Sex"?

In what ways does our culture push the lie of lust?

Why doesn't lust work to improve sexual relationships?

What are the consequences to marriage and relationships of buying into the lie of lust, porn, masturbation, etc?

How does porn/masturbation break the "smiley face/heart" system that God put in place to be the ultimate connector in marriage?

www.laughyourway.com

Why is it so critical that our teenagers hear this information about lust, porn and masturbation?

SCRIPTURE REFERENCES:

Proverbs 4:23
Above all else, guard your heart, for it is the wellspring of life. (NIV)

Song of Solomon 7:10
I belong to my lover, and his desire is for me. (NIV)

NOTES:

> *Life is short, and you love your wife, so enjoy being with her. This is what you are supposed to do as you struggle through life on this earth.*
>
> *Ecclesiastes 9:9*

CLIP 26: SCIENTIFIC FORMULA FOR THE BEST POSSIBLE SEX (17:37)

Why is exclusivity a turn on for women?

How and why does Mark's formula for the "Best Possible Sex" make more sense than what the so-called "experts" are saying is the key to great sex?

How has "imprinting on lust" led our culture to where we are today?

Why does the best possible sex result from married sex?

Why do you think God's plan for great sex is so rejected and ignored by our culture?

www.laughyourway.com

What is the result of ignoring a husband's sexual need?

If you need help with pornography and sexual issues, please visit our website, www.laughyourway.com. Under "Resources", click on "Sexual Addiction" to find out more about the Pure Online Program.

SCRIPTURE REFERENCES:

Proverbs 6:27-28
27 Can a man carry fire in his arms, and his clothes not be burned? 28 Can a man walk on hot coals, and his feet not be burned? (NLV)

Proverbs 9:17-18
17 Stolen water is sweet. And bread eaten in secret is pleasing. 18 But he does not know that the dead are there, and that the ones who visit her are in the bottom of hell. (NLV)

NOTES:

END OF SESSION PRAYER

GROUP PRAYER:

Father,
Thank you for the wisdom and truth You give us when we seek You. Help us to apply what we learn to our marriage to make our relationships all You intend them to be. Keep us ever mindful of the importance of making our spouse and our marriage a priority. Guard our hearts and minds against the things of the world that would come to try to steal and destroy. Help us to maintain an exclusive love and desire for our spouses. Hide the truth of what we are learning deep in our hearts to make us the husbands and wives You want us to be. Amen.

COUPLES PRAYER:

Father,
Thank you for the wisdom and truth You give us when we seek You. Help us to apply what we learn to our marriage to make our relationship all You intend it to be. Keep us ever mindful of the importance of making each other and our marriage a priority. Guard our hearts and minds against the things of the world that would come to try to steal and destroy. Help us to maintain an exclusive love and desire for one another. Hide the truth of what we are learning deep in our hearts to make us the husband and wife You want us to be. Amen

SESSION 11 - Score!

CLIP 27: SCORING POINTS MEN (11:19)

Men have a way of "thinking big". Why doesn't this work when scoring points?

Wives, why is it that the big things score the same number points as the simple things?

What kinds of small things can men do to score points with their wives?

Wives, if your husband followed Mark's plan of engaging you in meaningful conversation, would that be pleasing to you? Would your husband score points?

I belong to my lover, and his desire is for me.

Song of Solomon 7:10

www.laughyourway.com

SCRIPTURE REFERENCES:

Proverbs 11:17
A kind man benefits himself, but a cruel man brings trouble on himself. (NIV)

Ecclesiastes 9:9
Life is short, and you love your wife, so enjoy being with her. This is what you are supposed to do as you struggle through life on this earth. (CEV)

NOTES:

CLIP 28: SCORING POINTS WOMEN (4:29)

Why is it so critically important that wives believe in their husbands?

What things can a wife do to show her husband that she is his "number one fan"?

Men, how does it feel when your wife is supportive of you and validates you?

Why is harsh criticism so detrimental to most men?

SCRIPTURE REFERENCES:

Ephesians 5:22
Wives, understand and support your husbands in ways that show your support for Christ. (MSG)

1 Thessalonians 5:11
So encourage each other and build each other up, just as you are already doing. (NLT)

Can a man carry fire in his arms, and his clothes not be burned? Can a man walk on hot coals, and his feet not be burned?

Proverbs 6:27-28

---

www.laughyourway.com

NOTES:

END OF SESSION PRAYER

GROUP PRAYER:

*Father,
Bring us clear understanding of what we need to do to love and honor each other. Help us to build marriages that will glorify and honor You. Make us aware of the everyday, ordinary, little things that go far in building up our husbands and wives. Help us to speak life in our homes so our families and marriages would be a shining light of Your love to the world. Use us to show Your plan and design for what marriage is to those around us. Thank you for Your love and provision and strength as we grow and become the husbands and wives You are creating us to be. Amen.*

COUPLES PRAYER:

*Father,
Bring us clear understanding of what we need to do to love and honor each other. Help us to build a marriage that will glorify and honor You. Make us aware of the everyday, ordinary, little things that go far in building one another up. Help us to speak life in our home so our family and marriage would be a shining light of Your love to the world. Use us to show Your plan and design for what marriage is to those around us. Thank you for Your love and provision and strength as we grow and become the husband and wife You are creating us to be. Amen.*

www.laughyourway.com

SESSION 12 - Starting Over...Again

CLIP 29: RESET BUTTON (8:36)

What are some of the circumstances for which you wish you had a "reset button" in your life?

What would be the advantages to having a "reset button" in your marriage?

Mark says that we DO have a reset button in life. What do you think that is? How do you think it works?

SCRIPTURE REFERENCES:

Proverbs 19:11
A man's understanding makes him slow to anger. It is to his honor to forgive and forget a wrong done to him. (NLV)

Philippians 2:2
… fulfill my joy by thinking the same way, having the same love, sharing the same feelings, focusing on one goal. (CSB)

1 Peter 4:8
Above all, love each other deeply, because love covers over a multitude of sins. (NIV)

Love is not rude, it is not self-seeking, it is not easily angered, it keeps no record of wrongs.

1 Corinthians 13:5

www.laughyourway.com

NOTES:

CLIP 30: FORGIVENESS (2:45)

According to the definition Mark gave, what is forgiveness?

Why is forgiveness not optional?

What are the consequences of not forgiving?

How is forgiving different from forgetting?

What does Mark mean when he says you can choose to forgive? What benefits come with this choice?

www.laughyourway.com

SESSION 12 - STARTING OVER...AGAIN

SCRIPTURE REFERENCES:

Matthew 6:9-15
⁹"This, then, is how you should pray: " 'Our Father in heaven, hallowed be Your name, ¹⁰ Your kingdom come, Your will be done on earth as it is in heaven. ¹¹ Give us today our daily bread. ¹² Forgive us our debts, as we also have forgiven our debtors. ¹³ And lead us not into temptation, but deliver us from the evil one. ¹⁴ For if you forgive men when they sin against you, your heavenly Father will also forgive you. ¹⁵ But if you do not forgive men their sins, your Father will not forgive your sins. (NIV)

Matthew 18:32-35
³²"Then the master called the servant in. 'You wicked servant,' he said, 'I canceled all that debt of yours because you begged me to. ³³ Shouldn't you have had mercy on your fellow servant just as I had on you?' ³⁴ In anger his master turned him over to the jailers to be tortured, until he should pay back all he owed. ³⁵"This is how my heavenly Father will treat each of you unless you forgive your brother from your heart." (NIV)

Mark 11:25
And when you stand praying, if you hold anything against anyone, forgive him, so that your Father in heaven may forgive you your sins." (NIV)

NOTES:

Never pay back evil for evil to anyone. Do things in such a way that everyone can see you are honorable. Do your part to live in peace with everyone, as much as possible.

Romans 12:17-18

www.laughyourway.com

CLIP 31: BATHSHEBA (3:34)

Why is the story of Bathsheba included in the Bible?

What implication does this story have for our marriages?

What situations in your own life can you think of that the incredible power of forgiveness needs to be applied to?

SCRIPTURE REFERENCES:

2 Samuel 11
[1] In the spring, at the time when kings go off to war, David sent Joab out with the king's men and the whole Israelite army. They destroyed the Ammonites and besieged Rabbah. But David remained in Jerusalem.

[2] One evening David got up from his bed and walked around on the roof of the palace. From the roof he saw a woman bathing. The woman was very beautiful, [3] and David sent someone to find out about her. The man said, "Isn't this Bathsheba, the daughter of Eliam and the wife of Uriah the Hittite?"

[4] Then David sent messengers to get her. She came to him, and he slept with her. (She had purified herself from her uncleanness.) Then she went back home. [5] The woman conceived and sent word to David, saying, "I am pregnant."

www.laughyourway.com

⁶ So David sent this word to Joab: "Send me Uriah the Hittite." And Joab sent him to David. ⁷ When Uriah came to him, David asked him how Joab was, how the soldiers were and how the war was going. ⁸ Then David said to Uriah, "Go down to your house and wash your feet." So Uriah left the palace, and a gift from the king was sent after him. ⁹ But Uriah slept at the entrance to the palace with all his master's servants and did not go down to his house.

¹⁰ When David was told, "Uriah did not go home," he asked him, "Haven't you just come from a distance? Why didn't you go home?" ¹¹ Uriah said to David, "The ark and Israel and Judah are staying in tents, and my master Joab and my lord's men are camped in the open fields. How could I go to my house to eat and drink and lie with my wife? As surely as you live, I will not do such a thing!"

¹² Then David said to him, "Stay here one more day, and tomorrow I will send you back." So Uriah remained in Jerusalem that day and the next. ¹³ At David's invitation, he ate and drank with him, and David made him drunk. But in the evening Uriah went out to sleep on his mat among his master's servants; he did not go home. ¹⁴ In the morning David wrote a letter to Joab and sent it with Uriah.

¹⁵ In it he wrote, "Put Uriah in the front line where the fighting is fiercest. Then withdraw from him so he will be struck down and die."

¹⁶ So while Joab had the city under siege, he put Uriah at a place where he knew the strongest defenders were. ¹⁷ When the men of the city came out and fought against Joab, some of the men in David's army fell; moreover, Uriah the Hittite died.

¹⁸ Joab sent David a full account of the battle. ¹⁹ He instructed the messenger: "When you have finished giving the king this account of the battle, ²⁰ the king's anger may flare up, and he may ask you, 'Why did you get so close to the city to fight? Didn't you know they would shoot arrows from the wall?

²¹ Who killed Abimelech son of Jerub-Besheth? Didn't a woman throw an upper millstone on him from the wall, so that he died in Thebez? Why did you get so close to the wall?' If he asks you this, then say to him, 'Also, your servant Uriah the Hittite is dead.' " ²² The messenger set out, and when he arrived he told David everything Joab had sent him to say.

²³ The messenger said to David, "The men overpowered us and came out against us in the open, but we drove them back to the entrance to the city gate. ²⁴ Then the archers shot arrows at your servants from the wall, and some of the king's men died. Moreover, your servant Uriah the Hittite is dead." ²⁵ David told the messenger, "Say this to Joab: 'Don't let this upset you; the sword devours one as well as another. Press the attack against the city and destroy it.' Say this to encourage Joab."

²⁶ When Uriah's wife heard that her husband was dead, she mourned for him. ²⁷ After the time of mourning was over, David had her brought to his house, and she became his wife and bore him a son. But the thing David had done displeased the LORD. (NIV)

2 Samuel 12

[1] The LORD sent Nathan to David. When he came to him, he said, "There were two men in a certain town, one rich and the other poor. [2] The rich man had a very large number of sheep and cattle, [3] but the poor man had nothing except one little ewe lamb he had bought. He raised it, and it grew up with him and his children. It shared his food, drank from his cup and even slept in his arms. It was like a daughter to him.

[4] "Now a traveler came to the rich man, but the rich man refrained from taking one of his own sheep or cattle to prepare a meal for the traveler who had come to him. Instead, he took the ewe lamb that belonged to the poor man and prepared it for the one who had come to him."

[5] David burned with anger against the man and said to Nathan, "As surely as the LORD lives, the man who did this deserves to die! [6] He must pay for that lamb four times over, because he did such a thing and had no pity." [7] Then Nathan said to David, "You are the man! This is what the LORD, the God of Israel, says: 'I anointed you king over Israel, and I delivered you from the hand of Saul.

[8] I gave your master's house to you, and your master's wives into your arms. I gave you the house of Israel and Judah. And if all this had been too little, I would have given you even more. [9] Why did you despise the word of the LORD by doing what is evil in his eyes? You struck down Uriah the Hittite with the sword and took his wife to be your own. You killed him with the sword of the Ammonites. [10] Now, therefore, the sword will never depart from your house, because you despised me and took the wife of Uriah the Hittite to be your own.'

[11] "This is what the LORD says: 'Out of your own household I am going to bring calamity upon you. Before your very eyes I will take your wives and give them to one who is close to you, and he will lie with your wives in broad daylight. [12] You did it in secret, but I will do this thing in broad daylight before all Israel.' " [13] Then David said to Nathan, "I have sinned against the LORD." Nathan replied, "The LORD has taken away your sin. You are not going to die.

[14] But because by doing this you have made the enemies of the LORD show utter contempt, the son born to you will die." [15] After Nathan had gone home, the LORD struck the child that Uriah's wife had borne to David, and he became ill. [16] David pleaded with God for the child. He fasted and went into his house and spent the nights lying on the ground. [17] The elders of his household stood beside him to get him up from the ground, but he refused, and he would not eat any food with them. [18] On the seventh day the child died. David's servants were afraid to tell him that the child was dead, for they thought, "While the child was still living, we spoke to David but he would not listen to us. How can we tell him the child is dead? He may do something desperate." [19] David noticed that his servants were whispering among themselves and he realized the child was dead. "Is the child dead?" he asked. "Yes," they replied, "he is dead." [20] Then David got up from the ground. After he had washed, put on lotions and changed his clothes, he went into the house of the LORD and worshiped. Then he went to his own house, and at his request they served him food, and he ate.

[21] His servants asked him, "Why are you acting this way? While the child was alive,

you fasted and wept, but now that the child is dead, you get up and eat!" [22] He answered, "While the child was still alive, I fasted and wept. I thought, 'Who knows? The LORD may be gracious to me and let the child live.' [23] But now that he is dead, why should I fast? Can I bring him back again? I will go to him, but he will not return to me."

[24] Then David comforted his wife Bathsheba, and he went to her and lay with her. She gave birth to a son, and they named him Solomon. (NIV)

NOTES:

A gentle response defuses anger, but a sharp tongue kindles a temper-fire.

Proverbs 15:1

www.laughyourway.com

CLIP 32: PUSHING THE RESET BUTTON (2:47)

***Optional: While watching the DVD, stand facing your spouse, and repeat the words to each other as Mark reads them. ***

How is forgiveness the "reset button" of life?

Is forgiveness a one-time thing? How often should you forgive?

How easy is it for you to forgive?

What do you need to do in order to forgive your spouse?

How is the forgiveness statement Mark uses helpful to you?

www.laughyourway.com

SCRIPTURE REFERENCES:

Matthew 18:21-22
²¹ Then Peter came to Him and said, "Lord, how often shall my brother sin against me, and I forgive him? Up to seven times?" ²² Jesus said to him, "I do not say to you, up to seven times, but up to seventy times seven." (NKJ)

Romans 12:17-18
¹⁷ Never pay back evil for evil to anyone. So things in such a way that everyone can see you are honorable. ¹⁸ Do your part to live in peace with everyone, as much as possible. (NLT)

1 Corinthians 13:5
(Love) is not rude, it is not self-seeking, it is not easily angered, it keeps no record of wrongs. (NIV)

2 Corinthians 13:11
…Do that which makes you complete. Be comforted. Work to get along with others. Live in peace….(NLV)

Galatians 5:15
But if you hurt and make it hard for each other, watch out or you may be destroyed by each other. (NLV)

NOTES:

And when you stand praying, if you hold anything against anyone, forgive him, so that your Father in heaven may forgive you your sins.

Mark 11:25

www.laughyourway.com

END OF SESSION PRAYER

GROUP PRAYER:

Father,
Thank you for Your endless mercy, grace and forgiveness. Help us to always remember to extend that same forgiveness to others, especially in our marriages. Create in us a forgiving and merciful spirit so that we can let go of our hurt, anger and frustration - even when it is difficult.

We thank you for all of the wisdom, understanding and insight that we have gained during this time together. Bring us back to these principles and truths over and over again as we continue to grow into the husbands and wives You want us to be. May we become people who love and give selflessly and sacrificially, especially in our marriages. Bless each and every marriage represented here and bring other couples into our lives that will also be blessed through us. Thank you for Your almighty power and love and for allowing us to share that with the world around us. Amen.

COUPLES PRAYER:

Father,
Thank you for Your endless mercy, grace and forgiveness. Help us to always remember to extend that same forgiveness to others, especially in our marriage. Create in us a forgiving and merciful spirit so that we can let go of our hurt, anger and frustration - even when it is difficult.

We thank you for all of the wisdom, understanding and insight that we have gained during this time together. Bring us back to these principles and truths over and over again as we continue to grow into the husband and wife You want us to be. May we become people who love and give selflessly and sacrificially, especially to each other in our marriage. Bless our marriage and bring other couples into our lives that will also be blessed through us. Thank you for Your almighty power and love and for allowing us to share that with the world around us. Amen.

www.laughyourway.com

Pastor Mark and Debbie Gungor

Mark Gungor is the CEO of Laugh Your Way America and Senior Pastor of Celebration Church. Married to Debbie for more than 30 years, he is also the creator of the highly regarded Laugh Your Way to a Better Marriage® seminar. Mark believes that the key to a successful marriage is not about finding the right person; it's about doing the right things. If you do the right things you will succeed, if you don't, you'll fail. It's just that simple. Our goal is to help couples get along, get it right, have fun and achieve a successful marriage. Laugh Your Way America exists to eliminate divorce in America, one family at a time.

Laugh Your Way America!, LLC
3475 Humboldt Road
Green Bay, WI 54311
866-525-2844
www.laughyourway.com

Marriage and Family Resources from Mark Gungor and Laugh Your Way America

THE FLAG PAGE SOLUTION

Now that you've discovered your child's heart, it's time you discover the great things God has in store for you by creating your own Flag Page. The Flag Page is an incredible on-line program designed to help you discover who you are, what you love the most about life and most importantly…who God created you to be.

The entire assessment takes 10 minutes and is great for teens, parents, grandparents, co-workers… the list goes on and on. To get started, log onto www.flagpage.com. It's inexpensive, easy and life-changing.

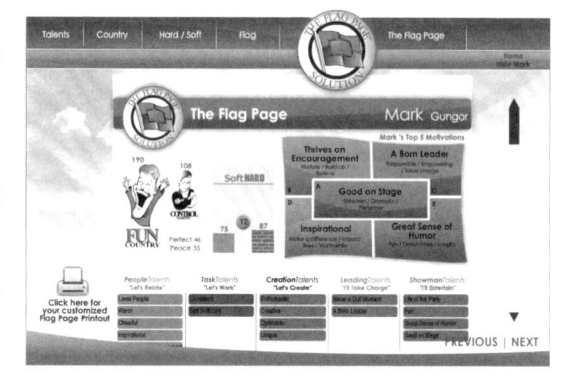

DISCOVERING YOUR HEART WITH THE FLAG PAGE

In his book Discovering Your Heart with the Flag Page, national marriage speaker Mark Gungor explains how to interpret and understand the colorful printout that is the Flag Page. He shows the reader how to understand why they act and react the way they do, and what important needs they have in their life that are the keys to their success and happiness.

Order your copy at www.laughyourway.com

www.flagpage.com

Marriage and Family Resources from Mark Gungor and Laugh Your Way America

LAUGH YOUR WAY TO A BETTER MARRIAGE

For the first time ever, the entire life-changing Laugh Your Way to a Better Marriage Event is available on DVD!

Filmed in Phoenix, Arizona, this 4-Disc DVD set includes every minute of Mark Gungor's weekend seminar, as well as an extra DVD featuring Mark answering the questions he couldn't cover during the original taping. With over 6 hours of material, the DVD set captures all the fun and facts of Mark's look at life, love, and marriage. Mark will walk you through from beginning to end as you laugh, learn and realize you can make immediate positive change in your own marriage. Perfect for couples, singles and youth, this set makes a great gift. From "The Tale of Two Brains" to the funny, hard-hitting, and must-hear information in "The Number One Key to Incredible Sex", Mark will have you laughing your way to a better marriage in no time!

SEX, DATING & RELATING - TEEN EDITION

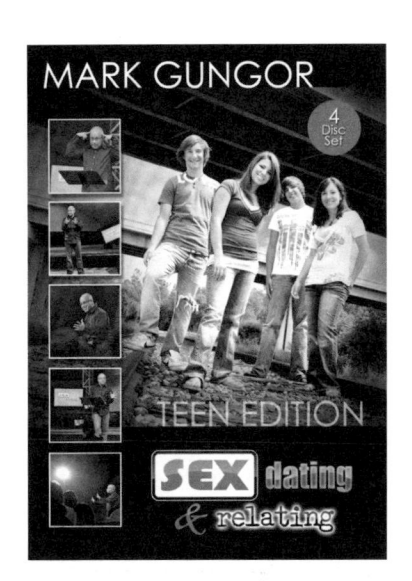

As Mark travels the country speaking on the subject of marriage, many have said, "I wish I'd known this when I was younger. Do you have this information for my kids or grandkids?"

Here is the highly anticipated and much sought after information on dating and sex that we all wish we had known growing up. In the society and culture we live in today, it is more important than ever that parents and teens are armed with the real facts and the truth. It's time to cut through all the nonsense that is taught in the media, the education system and even the Church.

Together, Mark and Pam Stenzel bring parents and teens the hard-hitting, no-nonsense wisdom not often heard in the secular or faith culture today. Messages that will help teens and their families make wise decisions enabling the next generation to build strong and successful marriages and families...without all the physical and emotional baggage.

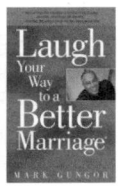

These and many more resources are all available at www.laughyourway.com

Listen to the Mark Gungor Show LIVE Monday - Friday from 10:00am - 11:00am Central Time. Join Mark as he discusses any and all issues concerning live, love and marriage.

www.markgungorshow.com

BIBLE TRANSLATIONS USED IN THE STUDY GUIDE

AMP - Scripture quotations taken from the Amplified® Bible, Copyright © 1954, 1958, 1962, 1964, 1965, 1987 by The Lockman Foundation Used by permission. (www.Lockman.org)

CEV - Scriptures marked as "(CEV)" are taken from the Contemporary English Version Copyright © 1995 by American Bible Society. Used by permission.

CSB - Scripture quotations are taken from the Holman Christian Standard Bible®, Copyright © 1999, 2000, 2002, 2003 by Holman Bible Publishers. Used by permission.

JPS - Jewish Publication Society Old Testament—Public Domain

MSG - Scripture taken from The Message. Copyright © 1993, 1994, 1995, 1996, 2000, 2001, 2002. Used by permission of NavPress Publishing Group.

NAB - Scripture texts in this work are taken from the New American Bible with Revised New Testament and Revised Psalms © 1991, 1986, 1970 Confraternity of Christian Doctrine, Washington, D.C. and are used by permission of the copyright owner. All Rights Reserved. No part of the New American Bible may be reproduced in any form without permission in writing from the copyright owner.

NASB - Scripture taken from the NEW AMERICAN STANDARD BIBLE®, Copyright © 1960,1962,1963,1968,1971,1972,1973,1975,1977,1995 by The Lockman Foundation. Used by permission.

NCV - Scriptures quoted from The Holy Bible, New Century Version, copyright © 1987, 1988, 1991 by Word Publishing, Nashville, Tennessee 37214. Used by permission.

NIV - Scripture taken from the HOLY BIBLE, NEW INTERNATIONAL VERSION®. Copyright © 1973, 1978, 1984 International Bible Society. Used by permission of Zondervan. All rights reserved.

NKJ - Scripture taken from the New King James Version. Copyright © 1982 by Thomas Nelson, Inc. Used by permission. All rights reserved.

NLT - Scripture quotations marked (NLT) are taken from the Holy Bible, New Living Translation, copyright © 1996. Used by permission of Tyndale House Publishers, Inc., Wheaton, Illinois 60189. All rights reserved.

NLV - Scripture taken from the Holy Bible, New Life Version, Copyright 1969, 1976, 1978, 1983, 1986, Christian Literature International, P. O. Box 777, Canby, OR 97013. Used by permission.

RSV - The Bible text designated RSV is from The Holy Bible: Revised Standard Version. Copyright 1946, 1952, 1959, 1973 by the Division of Christian Education of the National Council of the Churches of Christ in the United States of America. All rights reserved. Used by permission.

WEB - World English Bible - Public Domain

RESOURCES

Love & Respect: The Love She Most Desires, The Respect He Desperately Needs
by Emerson Eggerichs

The Five Love Languages
by Gary Chapman

The Flag Page
at www.flagpage.com

For Better or for Best
by Gary Smalley

If Only He Knew
by Gary Smalley

Every Woman's Desire - Every Man's Guide to Winning the Heart of a Woman
by Stephen Arterburn and Fred Stoeker

Wild at Heart
by John Eldredge

Men Are From Mars, Women Are From Venus
by John Gray

Sexual Intimacy in Marriage
by William Cutrer, MD and Sandra Glahn

The Smart Stepfamily
by Ron L. Deal